AI

The New Gold Rush

by
Don Edwards

AI

The New Gold Rush

Table of Contents

Introduction

In an era where technology evolves at an unprecedented pace, artificial intelligence (AI) stands as a transformative pillar reshaping industries and redefining the way we approach everyday tasks. Whether you're an aspiring entrepreneur, a freelancer seeking to enhance productivity, or a professional eager to elevate your career, integrating AI into your work can unlock a world of potential. This book is your guide to tapping into that potential and using AI as a catalyst for financial success.

AI is no longer just the realm of tech giants or futuristic fantasies; it is a powerful tool accessible to anyone willing to learn and adapt. From improving decision-making processes to automating repetitive tasks, the applications of AI are as diverse as they are impactful. Understanding how to leverage these technologies will not only provide a competitive edge but also open up new avenues for income generation and business innovation.

For many, the concept of AI may seem daunting, filled with jargon and complex algorithms. However, the journey to harness AI doesn't require you to become a data scientist overnight. It requires curiosity, a willingness to learn, and the strategic application of AI tools that align with your goals. This book aims to demystify AI, breaking down its components and presenting opportunities in a way that is accessible for all, regardless of technical background.

The landscape of AI is vast and dynamic, offering opportunities that weren't imaginable just a few years ago. Innovations in AI continue to expand boundaries, allowing entrepreneurs to create startups with unprecedented capabilities, freelancers to amplify their efficiency, and professionals to reinvent their skill sets. As you navigate through this book, you will discover how AI can be applied in various contexts, providing practical insights and actionable strategies to harness its full potential.

One of the most exciting aspects of AI is its democratizing nature. While advanced AI tools and solutions have traditionally been the domain of large corporations with significant resources, today's tools are increasingly user-friendly and accessible to small business owners and individuals. This shift allows more people to partake in the digital revolution, leveling the playing field and enabling diverse voices to contribute to innovation.

This book is structured to provide a comprehensive overview of AI, from understanding its key components and differences between machine learning and deep learning, to exploring the entrepreneurial opportunities it presents. You'll read about AI's role in enhancing freelance work, professional development, and how to monetize AI innovations effectively. Furthermore, amidst AI's numerous prospects, it's crucial to acknowledge the challenges and ethical considerations that accompany its widespread implementation.

Our goal is not only to educate but also to inspire. The stories and case studies presented throughout the chapters show that success with AI is achievable with the right mindset and approach. Whether it's launching a startup infused with AI or using AI tools to streamline and elevate your existing work processes, the potential for financial growth and efficiency gains is immense.

But how do you begin to weave AI into the fabric of your professional life? This book serves as a roadmap to guide you through your AI journey. By the end of this exploration, you will have a clearer understanding of the AI landscape and be equipped with the knowledge to integrate AI into your business strategy. More importantly, you'll be prepared to look at AI not just as a tool, but as an innovative partner in reaching your financial goals.

So, as we embark on this exploration of AI's immense capabilities and opportunities, remember that the key to success lies not only in understanding technology but also in the vision to apply it creatively and ethically. The future is AI-enabled, and by embracing this future, you're positioning yourself to be at the forefront of a technological wave that continues to shape our world for the better.

Chapter 1:
Understanding the AI Landscape

Diving into the vast realm of artificial intelligence, you'll find that understanding the AI landscape is essential for anyone looking to leverage its potential for financial growth. AI isn't just a buzzword; it's rapidly reshaping industries and creating new opportunities for innovation. This first chapter sets the stage, introducing key concepts and components of AI technology that are transforming the way we work and do business. By grasping the foundations of algorithms and distinguishing between machine learning and deep learning, aspiring entrepreneurs, freelancers, and professionals can position themselves ahead of the curve. The aim here is to unravel the basic framework of AI, equipping you with the insight needed to explore its capabilities and apply them effectively in your ventures. As you navigate through this landscape, you'll start to see the myriad ways AI can propel you towards your financial goals.

Key Components of AI

Understanding the essential elements of AI is crucial for leveraging its transformative power in any business setting. At its core, AI consists of foundational components like data, algorithms, and computing power, each playing a unique role in the system's functionality. Data serves as the fuel, feeding AI systems the information they need to learn and make decisions. Algorithms act as the brains, processing this data to identify patterns and drive intelligent actions. Meanwhile, computing power ensures these processes occur efficiently and at a scale that matches real-world demands. Grasping these components isn't just technical; it's strategic. For aspiring entrepreneurs and professionals seeking to harness AI for financial growth, recognizing how these pieces interact can illuminate pathways to innovation and opportunity, setting the stage for future success.

Importance of Algorithms in AI

Understanding the landscape of artificial intelligence (AI) is essential, particularly when considering its key components. One such foundational element is algorithms. Think of algorithms as the backbone of AI—they're the detailed, step-by-step processes that guide AI systems through their tasks. Without algorithms, AI, as we know it, wouldn't exist. Algorithms enable AI systems to learn, make decisions, and solve complex problems, all of which are crucial for anyone looking to integrate AI into their work for financial growth.

For aspiring entrepreneurs and professionals, getting a firm grasp on the importance of algorithms can be a game-changer. Algorithms are what drive machine learning models, powering everything from predictive analytics to autonomous vehicles. They help transform raw data into insightful information, enabling AI to perform a variety of tasks based on the patterns and trends it extracts from that data. This ability to learn and adapt is what makes AI such a powerful tool in the modern economy.

The entrepreneurial potential of algorithms is vast. If you're venturing into AI-driven startups or wanting to optimize business operations, understanding algorithms can give you a significant edge. Let's consider the example of recommendation systems. These are used by giants like Amazon and Netflix to analyze user behavior and suggest products or content the user might like. The underlying algorithms consider numerous factors, such as past activities, preferences, and even the behavior of similar users, to provide personalized experiences.

Algorithms are not just about understanding data; they're about predicting future outcomes. This predictive capability is particularly appealing to industries focused on financial growth. For instance, financial institutions use algorithms to predict stock market trends, assess risks, and detect fraud. By harnessing these predictive powers, businesses can fine-tune their strategies, optimize performance, and improve their bottom line.

There is an inspirational aspect to algorithms as well. They simulate different ways to tackle challenges, offering an expansive toolkit for problem-solving. Entrepreneurs and freelancers who can master these tools are better positioned to innovate, creating solutions that address market demands or even unexpressed needs. Creative uses of algorithms could lead to the development of unique products and services that captivate consumers and secure a competitive advantage.

An algorithm's flexibility is one of its most attractive features. Depending on your specific needs, you can tailor algorithms to suit different applications. In AI and machine learning, algorithms can be supervised, unsupervised, or reinforcement-based depending on the type of learning required. This variety allows for customization in approaches to solving business problems, making algorithms applicable across different fields and industries.

Moreover, the understanding of algorithms can drive collaboration across disciplines. Engineers, data scientists, and business leaders all must communicate effectively to develop and deploy AI solutions efficiently. A common understanding of how algorithms work helps facilitate this collaboration, ensuring that everyone is aligned in achieving the company's financial objectives.

As AI continues to evolve, new algorithms are constantly being developed, pushing the boundaries of what's possible. With the ability to process enormous data sets faster and more efficiently, these algorithms become fundamental tools in the quest for innovation. AI entrepreneurs and professionals who keep abreast of these developments are better equipped to leverage them for financial growth.

Algorithms are not just theoretical constructs; they have practical applications that directly impact the market. For example, sentiment analysis algorithms can process customer review data to provide insights into consumer opinions and feedback. Companies can use this information to refine their products, improve customer satisfaction, and ultimately drive sales.

On a broader scale, algorithms powered by AI are pivotal in shaping future societies. From enhancing personalized education and healthcare diagnostics to enabling smarter city infrastructures, the reach of algorithms is expansive. Those looking to enter these fields must appreciate the nuances of algorithmic design and execution, as these are central to creating meaningful and impactful AI-driven solutions.

It's crucial to appreciate the ethical considerations when developing and implementing algorithms. Bias in algorithms can lead to unfair practices and decisions, potentially harming individuals or groups. Thus, entrepreneurs and professionals need to prioritize ethical integrity, ensuring their algorithms are fair, transparent, and accountable. Addressing these concerns not only builds trust with users but also enhances the long-term viability of AI applications.

In conclusion, understanding the importance of algorithms in AI is imperative for those seeking to leverage AI for financial success. With their wide-ranging applications and ability to transform industries, algorithms serve as an essential pillar in the architecture of

AI systems. As AI technologies continue to evolve, so will the algorithms that fuel them, making them a consistent focal point for innovation and growth.

Machine Learning vs. Deep Learning emerges as a pivotal distinction when exploring the AI landscape. Aspiring entrepreneurs, freelancers, and professionals often grapple with these terms, unsure of how each can contribute to financial success. Let's break down these concepts, focusing on their unique characteristics and why they're central to understanding AI's key components.

At its core, Machine Learning (ML) involves algorithms that allow computers to find patterns in data and make decisions without explicit instructions. This facet of AI is all about teaching machines using data instead of direct programming. For many startups, this capability is the first step into automating and scaling operations. Machine learning algorithms, like decision trees, linear regression, and support vector machines, play a critical role in processing vast amounts of information and extracting actionable insights.

On the other hand, Deep Learning (DL) is a subset of machine learning, distinguished by its use of neural networks with many layers—hence the term "deep." These networks attempt to mimic the human brain's neural architecture, adding complexity and capability to AI systems. Because of this intricate structure, deep learning can handle massive amounts of unstructured data, including images and natural language, more effectively than traditional ML approaches.

Why does this matter to you, an entrepreneur looking to integrate AI into your work? The choice between machine learning and deep learning is crucial for shaping your AI strategy. Machine learning solutions often require less computational power and can be deployed more quickly for certain applications, making them ideal for projects with limited initial resources. This is why you might find it beneficial to employ machine learning in the early stages of business development to build strong data analytics capabilities without the burden of hefty investments in technology infrastructure.

Meanwhile, deep learning opens doors to more advanced possibilities. It powers innovations like self-driving car technology and sophisticated image recognition systems, which can revolutionize industries with high levels of automation and precision. However, if you're working with a large dataset and need top-tier accuracy, deep learning can be the more effective approach, provided you have access to considerable computing resources and data to train these extensive networks.

It's essential to recognize that both machine learning and deep learning depend on high-quality data. For entrepreneurs, freelancers, and professionals, understanding data's value is key. Machine learning models require well-curated datasets to perform optimally, while deep learning thrives on vast and often labeled datasets. This means investing in data collection and preprocessing is crucial, as it enhances model performance and, ultimately, the quality of decisions driven by AI.

The implementation of machine learning and deep learning can differ significantly. While ML models are often easier to interpret, giving you clear insights into how decisions are made, DL models can act as black boxes, offering less transparency into the decision-making process. For businesses prioritizing transparency, ML might be the preferred option. However, if the goal is to achieve high accuracy with less concern for understanding the model's inner workings, DL could serve better, especially in environments where results are more critical than the interpretability of these results.

Think of machine learning as a foundational tool for gaining competitive advantage. By maximizing the efficiency of existing processes, ML can help you discover patterns that inform strategic decisions, from improving customer experiences to optimizing supply chains. In contrast, deep learning holds the promise of transformative innovation. It can generate entirely new product offerings and business models by unlocking capabilities in computer vision, natural language processing, and more.

The practical application of these technologies is vast. For freelancers incorporating AI, machine learning can automate mundane tasks, allowing more time for creative and strategic thinking. Meanwhile, deep learning can help tackle complex problems, like developing custom AI models tailored to client specifications.

The difference between ML and DL also influences the skills required for successful implementation. A strong understanding of statistics, programming, and data handling is essential for both. However, deep learning often requires an additional layer of expertise in neural networks and model tuning, which can be a barrier but also an opportunity for those ready to invest time into mastering these skills. As AI training resources become more available, this knowledge gap is closing, making it more accessible for newcomers to delve into the deeper aspects of AI.

Integrating either machine learning or deep learning into business strategies offers ample pathways to financial growth. By adopting AI technologies, you unlock possibilities to not only streamline operations but also differentiate yourself in a crowded market and create value through innovation. For professionals keen on staying ahead, the ability to identify when and how to leverage ML and DL processes will be a determining factor in long-term success.

While there's often an overlap in their capabilities, the decision to use machine learning vs. deep learning should always align with desired outcomes, available resources, and the nature of the problem at hand. As you consider how to integrate these technologies into your projects, it's vital to remain adaptable—AI is an ever-evolving field, and staying informed about the latest advancements can provide you a strategic edge.

Ultimately, by synthesizing the potential of both machine learning and deep learning, and understanding their respective strengths and limitations, entrepreneurs, freelancers, and professionals can harness the power of AI. It's not just about keeping pace with technological change but about leveraging these technologies to drive financial success and pave the way for future innovations.

Chapter 2:
Opportunities in AI for Entrepreneurs

For today's entrepreneurs, the AI revolution isn't just a passing trend—it's a treasure trove of possibilities. Leveraging AI, they can drive innovation, disrupt industries, and unlock new value propositions that were unimaginable a few years ago. Entrepreneurs are uniquely positioned to identify gaps in the market and harness AI to fill them, offering smarter solutions and personalized experiences that customers crave. Venturing into AI doesn't mean reinventing the wheel; it's about augmenting business vision with cutting-edge technology. Whether you're launching a new startup or exploring ways to invigorate an existing business, understanding the potential of AI can significantly impact your competitive edge. While the initial steps might seem daunting, the myriad AI tools available today can simplify integration, ensuring that even the less tech-savvy can successfully engage with these technologies. The AI startup environment is ripe, yet it's the strategic application and unique insights of each entrepreneur that turn potential into profit. This era of AI is not just about creating more efficient businesses; it's about fostering innovative ecosystems that transcend traditional boundaries. Seize the opportunity and let AI be the catalyst for your entrepreneurial journey.

The AI Startup Environment

The AI startup environment is a dynamic, fast-evolving landscape that's ripe with opportunities for entrepreneurs eager to make their mark. As AI technologies advance at a rapid pace, the barriers to entry for startups are lower than ever. Budding entrepreneurs can benefit from a growing ecosystem of accelerators, investors, and mentors who are keen to back innovative AI solutions. The drive for creating disruptive technologies has never been stronger, and with AI at the helm, startups have the potential to revolutionize industries ranging from healthcare to finance. The key for entrepreneurs is to remain agile, continuously learning and adapting to leverage the latest AI advancements. While competition is fierce, those who manage to carve out a niche will find that there are abundant opportunities to transform novel ideas into thriving businesses.

Case Studies of Successful AI Startups In the dynamic AI startup environment, many companies have carved out significant success by leveraging innovative technology and astute market strategies. Take for example, OpenAI, a firm that has redefined natural language processing through its development of language models. While its technology underpins a wide array of applications—from customer service bots to content creation tools—their secret lies not only in ingenious algorithms but also in their relentless focus on practicality and accessibility. They understood early on that building partnerships with established companies could amplify their reach, a strategy that continues to bear fruit.

Another noteworthy player, UiPath, emerged as a leader in robotic process automation (RPA). Their success story is particularly inspiring due to their focus on democratizing technology, making complex automation accessible to businesses of all sizes. By simplifying the user experience, they created a product that didn't demand extensive programming knowledge, thus widening their target audience

13

significantly. This approach allowed them to address a common challenge for many businesses—streamlining workflows without additional burdens.

Then there's the example of Assistance Intelligence. This startup took a different tack by focusing on niche markets. Rather than competing directly with tech giants, they specialized in AI solutions for healthcare diagnostics, an area desperately needing innovation. Their strategy of concentrating on a sector-specific problem not only made them indispensable to their clients but also shielded them from the fierce competition in broader fields. By addressing unique pain points with tailored solutions, they demonstrated the potential for startups to succeed on focused but impactful fronts.

Similarly, another remarkable success story is that of Grammarly, an AI-powered tool that revolutionized writing assistance. By progressively improving its natural language processing capabilities, Grammarly became a ubiquitous tool for both individuals and enterprises. The key to its triumph was its continuous commitment to enhancing user experience and expanding functionality, which included integrating with other platforms users frequented. By listening to customer feedback and iterating accordingly, they cemented a strong customer base, proving that user-centric development is a powerful growth catalyst.

In the realm of voice technology, Speechly has emerged as a promising startup with its unique take on facilitating more natural and effective voice interactions. The company capitalized on the growing demand for voice-enabled experiences by offering superior voice recognition technology that could be easily embedded into software solutions. Focusing on seamless integration and multi-language support opened up diverse international markets, aligning with the global push towards more inclusive tech solutions. Their pragmatic approach to product development offers vital lessons in adaptability and foresight.

Additionally, consider the case of DataRobot, a company that has transformed the way organizations approach machine learning. By creating an automated machine learning platform, they empowered businesses to build and deploy AI models with unprecedented ease. This move democratized access to high-level machine learning capabilities, similar to UiPath's impact on process automation. DataRobot illustrates that democratization in technology not only breaks down barriers but also increases adoption, which is crucial for any startup looking to scale rapidly.

Furthermore, in the fintech sector, the impact of AI innovations can be seen through the triumphs of companies like Sentient Technologies. They leveraged AI to revolutionize how investment decisions are made, providing data-driven insights that far exceed human analytical capabilities. The financial gains afforded by such technologies didn't merely provide their target market with better tools—they drastically altered the competitive landscape for investment management, highlighting the transformative power AI holds across industries.

Another extraordinary illustration is the AI startup Cognitivescale, which specializes in developing trusted AI systems across different sectors, from healthcare to financial services. Their success rests on a sharp focus on enhancing transparency and accountability in AI systems, tackling one of the most significant hurdles faced in AI deployment today. By aligning their core values with widespread industry concerns, they established themselves as thought leaders in ethical AI, which significantly bolstered their credibility and market position.

Lastly, let's touch on how NORTH, an AI startup, used technology to elevate consumer experiences in the retail and e-commerce sectors. By harnessing AI to improve personalization and customer engagement strategies, NORTH offered businesses insights into buyer behaviors that were previously unattainable. Their focus on enhancing consumer interaction illustrates how AI startups can thrive by empowering others to achieve meaningful, measurable improvements in end-user satisfaction.

As we've seen, the common thread in these case studies is the ability of AI startups to identify specific problems and offer bespoke solutions that resonate with their target markets. From democratization and transparency to specialization and user-centric designs, these strategies have provided not only a competitive edge but also a sustainable path to growth. Entrepreneurs entering the AI landscape should consider these exemplars as blueprints, adapting lessons to suit their unique contexts and ambitions while championing AI's transformative potential.

Chapter 3:
AI Applications in Freelancing

The freelancing landscape is evolving rapidly, with AI at the helm of this transformation, offering unprecedented opportunities for those willing to embrace it. For freelancers, the integration of AI tools can reshape how work is managed and delivered, driving efficiency and innovation. Imagine a world where routine tasks are automated, freeing up time to focus on creative and strategic endeavors that add real value to clients. AI can assist in tasks ranging from content creation to data analysis, each enhancing a freelancer's toolkit. By adopting AI, freelancers aren't just improving productivity; they're setting themselves apart in a competitive market, positioning themselves as forward-thinking professionals ready to leverage technology for superior results. This chapter will explore these AI applications, illustrating how they can redefine freelance work and pave the way for financial success.

Freelancers' Guide to AI Tools

Diving into the world of freelancing with AI tools can be a game-changer, unlocking new pathways to efficiency and creativity. AI tools help streamline daily tasks, from scheduling to data analysis, giving you more time to focus on higher-value projects that create significant opportunities for growth. As freelance professionals, you'll find AI can assist with content creation, design, or automation, allowing you to enhance your service offerings without increasing your workload. Many tools are designed with freelancers in mind, offering scalable solutions that fit both your skill level and budget. By embracing these technologies, freelancers can not only keep pace with industry changes but also lead the charge, turning AI from a mysterious buzzword into a powerful partner in achieving sustained financial success.

Maximizing Productivity with Automation is more than just a fancy catchphrase; it's a necessity for freelancers in today's fast-paced digital world. Embracing AI-powered automation can be the edge you need to compete in the chaotic gig economy. Automation isn't about replacing creativity or reducing the human element in your work. Instead, it's about amplifying your abilities, allowing you to focus on the tasks that truly require your unique skill set.

Let's start by understanding what automation can do for you as a freelancer. Think of the mundane, repetitive tasks that tend to chew up your time—things like scheduling posts, managing client communications, or organizing files. AI tools can handle these with remarkable efficiency, freeing up your time for more strategic and creative work. By delegating routine tasks to AI, you can focus on what's genuinely value-adding.

Take email management, for instance. AI can now sift through your inbox to prioritize messages, respond with pre-set templates for common inquiries, and even detect sentiment to alert you to more urgent messages. The boost to productivity is evident, allowing you to engage with clients meaningfully, instead of sorting through clutter. Over time, this heightened efficiency can lead to increased client satisfaction and potentially more business.

But it's not just about task automation. AI tools can analyze data to generate insights, providing freelancers with key decisions faster than ever before. Machine learning algorithms are increasingly adept at turning vast quantities of information into actionable insights with applications ranging from market research to project management. Picture the advantage of having a tool that could predict client needs or trending topics in your area of expertise.

Consider AI-powered content creation as another illustration. Tools that automate writing can generate drafts at incredible speed, allowing you to take on more projects without compromising quality. While a human touch is necessary for the final polish, these AI tools give a significant head start, giving you more bandwidth to juggle multiple commissions.

Automation also plays a pivotal role in project management. AI-powered platforms offer features like smart task prioritization and deadline forecasting. Gone are the days of manually updating project timelines or setting reminders. The AI anticipates your workflow needs, suggesting adjustments to keep projects on track and stress levels down.

Streamlining client interactions is another area where AI shines. Chatbots and AI-driven communication tools allow for instant replies, setting expectations promptly, and even scheduling meetings automatically. Automated invoicing systems ensure you never miss billing a client while AI-driven analytics can help you track payment trends or identify late payers.

Moreover, integrating automation into your freelancing workflow can enhance collaboration if you're working as part of a team or with clients who have their AI systems. Compatibility and interoperability become less of a challenge, allowing for seamless data exchange and more fluid project execution. AI can act as a translator, turning data from various systems into a unified format that you can easily interpret and use.

It's essential to keep in mind, though, that implementation needs a thoughtful approach. Jumping on every new AI tool can lead to an overwhelmed system, which might diminish productivity instead of enhancing it. Instead, focus on integrating tools that align closely with your specific needs and work habits. Start small, test extensively, and scale as you become more comfortable and proficient.

Even as AI takes over repetitive tasks, freelancers should focus on continuous learning. Understanding how to maximize these tools will ensure they remain relevant and competitive. Many online courses and communities offer resources to help you understand AI's capabilities and how to wield them effectively, making this a lifelong learning journey that's both rewarding and essential.

Looking ahead, imagine a future where almost every aspect of freelancing is streamlined, allowing you even greater freedom to explore expansive projects or diversify your skill set without the burden of minutiae. The ultimate goal of maximization through automation is to give you the power to focus solely on your zone of genius.

Incorporating AI into your freelance endeavors is not just a trend but a transformation that empowers you to reclaim your time and refine your craft. In this unfolding AI-enhanced freelancing landscape, the tools you choose can distinguish you as not just a participant but a leader who leverages intelligence to its fullest potential. Use automation to work smarter, not harder, and witness how it takes your freelance career to uncharted heights.

Chapter 4:
AI in Professional Development

In today's fast-evolving professional landscape, integrating AI into your career path can be a game-changer. Professionals across various fields are turning to AI to enhance their skill sets and redefine what it means to excel in their roles. AI provides an array of powerful tools and resources that not only streamline workflow but also offer unique learning opportunities. By leveraging AI-driven training programs, professionals can acquire new competencies and stay ahead of industry trends. It's about embracing the potential of AI to transform routine tasks into innovative processes, allowing more space for creativity and strategic thinking. This chapter delves into how utilizing AI for skill enhancement can be pivotal for anyone seeking growth, not just in terms of expertise but also in achieving meaningful career advancement. As we explore this transformative journey, remember, embracing AI is about enhancing human potential rather than replacing it.

Enhancing Skill Sets with AI

As AI technology reshapes industries, professionals are finding new ways to enhance their skill sets by integrating AI into their daily routines. This transformation isn't just about adopting new tools; it's about cultivating a mindset that embraces constant change and innovation. AI empowers professionals to automate mundane tasks, allowing them to focus on strategic and creative endeavors that drive career growth. Engaging with AI tools can significantly enhance analytical, problem-solving, and decision-making skills. By proactively learning and adapting to AI developments, individuals position themselves to thrive in an increasingly AI-driven world. This journey can be exciting, as it transforms not only how we work but also how we envision our potential and career paths.

Leveraging Online AI Courses is a powerful strategy when it comes to enhancing skill sets with AI. Recognizing the vast potential of AI, professionals across industries are seeking ways to integrate this technology into their work. Online courses offer a flexible and accessible route to acquiring AI knowledge, making them an invaluable resource for entrepreneurs and freelancers eager to harness AI for financial success.

Online AI courses have democratized learning, removing geographical and financial barriers that once restricted access to quality education. With a stable internet connection, anyone can tap into resources from renowned institutions and industry experts. This accessibility allows learners to tailor their educational experience according to their schedules and learning paces. Flexible and self-directed, these courses empower individuals to learn and apply AI concepts at their convenience, making it easier than ever to integrate AI into their professional toolkits.

AI courses online range from basic introductions to complex algorithm development. A beginner might start with an overview of AI principles, progressing through modules that cover machine learning, data processing, and neural networks. More advanced courses delve into specialized topics like natural language processing or computer vision. Such breadth ensures that learners can find courses matching their current proficiency and career goals, enabling a continuum of skill enhancement.

One of the standout features of online AI courses is their emphasis on practical application. Rather than just theoretical knowledge, these courses often involve hands-on projects that mirror real-world problems. By working on these projects, learners accumulate tangible experience, which is critical for effectively implementing AI in professional settings. Such a pragmatic approach not only boosts learners' confidence but also builds a portfolio of work showcasing their capabilities to prospective clients or employers.

Moreover, online AI courses frequently incorporate community interaction through forums or peer collaboration. These platforms promote the exchange of ideas and solutions, allowing learners to benefit from diverse perspectives. Engaging with a community of like-minded individuals can be incredibly motivating, inspiring learners to push the boundaries of their knowledge and strive for excellence. This collaborative environment also mimics real-world professional scenarios, where AI solutions are often developed by interdisciplinary teams.

From a financial perspective, investing in online AI courses can yield substantial returns. As AI continues to permeate various industries, the demand for skilled professionals will only rise. By proactively building AI expertise, learners position themselves as competitive candidates for roles that require AI proficiency. They can command higher salaries, consulting fees, or create innovative AI-driven products and services that meet market demands.

Entrepreneurs and freelancers can also leverage AI courses to identify new business opportunities. By understanding the nuances of AI technologies, they can brainstorm unique applications that address unmet needs in their fields. This insight can lead to the creation of niche AI products or services, further enhancing their market value and profitability.

Platforms like Coursera, edX, and Udacity offer AI courses crafted by top-tier universities and tech companies. Recognized certificates from these institutions can bolster a professional profile, providing a tangible demonstration of one's commitment to continuous learning and expertise in AI. It's important to assess the course offerings and choose programs that provide comprehensive content, skilled instructors, and opportunities for real-world application.

Ultimately, leveraging online AI courses as a tool for professional development is about embracing change and staying ahead of the curve. AI is not just a tool; it's a transformative force reshaping industries and job roles. By investing time and resources into mastering AI through online courses, professionals can not only enhance their skills but also unlock new avenues for financial growth and career advancement.

Chapter 5:
Monetizing AI Innovations

In the swiftly evolving world of AI, the potential to transform groundbreaking ideas into lucrative ventures is unprecedented. Entrepreneurs, freelancers, and professionals keen on harnessing these technological advances must strategically navigate the monetization landscape. Key to success is understanding how to create AI-driven products that address genuine market needs while employing effective monetization strategies. Options range from subscription models and licensing agreements to providing premium features or services that offer tangible value. However, tapping into this goldmine demands a thoughtful approach—balancing innovation with customer-centric designs that ensure appeal and sustainability. As AI continues to reshape industries, those who can blend its capabilities with entrepreneurial savvy are poised to achieve significant financial growth, all while paving the path for future advancements.

Creating AI-Driven Products

Diving into the realm of AI-driven products is a thrilling venture for any entrepreneur eager to harness the power of cutting-edge technology for financial success. The creation of these products begins with identifying problems that AI can uniquely solve, thereby carving out a niche where innovation can thrive. It's about thinking beyond conventional solutions, leveraging AI's capabilities to offer distinct value and enhance user experience. This journey requires a blend of creativity, technical prowess, and a deep understanding of market needs. As you develop these products, focus on scalability and adaptability to meet the dynamic demands of your target audience. Remember, successful AI-driven products often lie at the intersection of advanced technology and user-centric design, making them not only technologically feasible but also commercially viable. By embracing this approach, you'll be set to transform cutting-edge concepts into tangible realities that fuel growth and capture the imagination of consumers worldwide.

Monetization Strategies for AI Services In today's rapidly evolving digital landscape, AI-driven products offer myriad opportunities for entrepreneurs looking to capitalize on cutting-edge technology. To succeed in transforming your AI innovations into revenue-generating services, you need a strategic approach that aligns with your business goals. Whether you're building a standalone AI application or integrating AI into existing platforms, understanding the various ways to monetize your creations is crucial.

Start with understanding your market. Identifying potential customers and their pain points can lead to successful AI solutions. For instance, if you're working with natural language processing, targeting industries like customer service, healthcare, or finance might yield valuable use cases. Once you've identified the demand, fine-tuning your AI service to meet specific needs can greatly enhance its marketability.

One effective strategy is to offer tiered pricing models. These allow you to reach diverse customer segments by offering varying levels of services. A freemium model, where basic services are offered for free and advanced features come at a premium, is an excellent way to entice users while showcasing the value of your AI solutions. As users experience the benefits, many will be inclined to upgrade to paid plans, thus gradually increasing your revenue stream.

Another promising avenue is subscription-based models. This approach offers a steady income stream, allowing for better financial planning and resource allocation. Customers who pay a regular fee for access to your AI services provide you with predictable cash flow. To boost attractiveness, provide options for monthly, quarterly, or annual subscriptions and offer incentives, like discounts or additional features, for longer commitments.

Licensing could also be a viable option for your AI services. By allowing other businesses to use your technology with a licensing agreement, you generate a steady revenue without the need to manage every end user directly. Licensing is particularly effective for AI innovations in niche markets, where specialized AI capabilities can be integrated into third-party products.

For those creating AI-driven platforms, consider implementing transaction-based monetization. This strategy is common in AI services facilitating trades or exchanges, such as marketplaces or financial trading platforms. Each transaction processed through your AI tool could yield a commission or fee. This model closely ties your earnings to the platform's activity, incentivizing you to grow the volume and scale of transactions.

Moreover, advertising can contribute effectively to monetizing AI services, especially in the digital content and media sectors. Engaging with advertisers looking to target specific audiences can turn your AI platform into a valuable ad space. AI's ability to analyze and predict user behavior enhances the effectiveness of targeted ads, allowing you to charge premium rates for more precise audience reach.

In some cases, providing AI as a consultancy service can be a lucrative monetization strategy. By offering bespoke AI solutions tailored to individual client needs, consultants can command higher fees. This model works well if your AI capabilities provide unique insights or decision-making tools for businesses seeking competitive advantage.

Make sure to explore partnerships and integrations with other companies. Collaborative efforts often bring mutual benefits, such as expanded customer bases and shared technological advancements. Partnering with established firms can lend credibility to your AI service, making it more appealing to cautious buyers.

Finally, consider leveraging data monetization if applicable. AI systems that collect and analyze large volumes of data have the potential to offer valuable insights as a service. By anonymizing and packaging these insights, you can create offerings that support data-driven decision-making in industries ranging from retail to public health.

Ultimately, your choice of monetization strategy should reflect the unique strengths and capabilities of your AI innovations. By aligning your business model with your technology's potential and market needs, you stand the best chance of achieving sustainable growth and financial success in the AI sector.

Chapter 6:
Real-Life AI Success Stories

In the world of AI, real-life success stories serve as powerful testaments to the transformative potential of technology in various industries. Consider the entrepreneur who revamped a traditional logistics company by implementing AI-driven predictive analytics, resulting in a significant reduction in fuel costs and delivery times. There's the freelancer who harnessed the power of machine learning to streamline data analysis, enabling unparalleled efficiency and attracting more clients. Similarly, a professional might leverage AI tools to personalize customer experiences on a massive scale, driving greater engagement and higher sales. These narratives not only showcase the diverse applications of AI but also inspire a new wave of innovation among those eager to unlock AI's financial benefits. Such stories illuminate the path to success, encouraging aspiring entrepreneurs and professionals to embrace AI and redefine the possibilities within their fields.

Entrepreneurs Transforming Businesses

In today's dynamic business world, entrepreneurs are seizing the power of AI to turn traditional business models on their heads. These visionary leaders aren't just keeping pace with technology—they're shaping the future by integrating AI into every facet of their companies. They're finding innovative solutions to age-old problems, from automating repetitive tasks to enhancing customer interaction with intelligent systems. By leveraging AI, they're driving efficiency and uncovering new revenue streams, creating a competitive edge that was once unimaginable. Whether it's through predictive analytics that redefine market strategies or machine learning systems that personalize the user experience, entrepreneurs are harnessing AI to elevate their businesses and inspire a new wave of economic growth. Their journeys highlight the endless possibilities AI offers and serve as a blueprint for aspiring leaders ready to transform their industries.

Success Story Analysis sets the stage to explore real-life instances of entrepreneurs who have successfully harnessed the power of Artificial Intelligence to revolutionize their businesses. In this dynamic and ever-growing sector, innovators are continually setting new benchmarks for success. What's fascinating is how these visionary leaders integrate AI to not just solve problems, but to rethink the very foundation of their industries.

Successful AI-driven transformations in business are a goldmine of insights and strategies for those looking to tread a similar path. One can't help but notice the common threads among these entrepreneurial stories: embracing data, experimenting with algorithms, and daring to disrupt traditional methodologies. These success stories emphasize clarity of vision, persistence, and a strong driving purpose. Consider a retail startup that's reinvented customer engagement using AI-driven insights. By analyzing mountains of consumer data, they've created personalized shopping experiences that have significantly boosted sales and customer loyalty.

Let's dive deeper into the transformation of a mid-sized manufacturing company that adopted AI to refine its supply chain and production processes. Traditionally, this meant relying on data from multiple disjointed systems leading to inefficiencies. By deploying an AI-enabled system, the company achieved real-time visibility across its operations, slashing costs and dramatically improving product delivery times. What stands out here is not merely the deployment of AI for automation but the strategic decision to use it to predict and solve future challenges proactively. This foresight was the game-changer.

Another compelling example is from the healthcare industry, where a startup leveraged AI to develop early detection systems for diseases. With the ability to analyze complex medical datasets rapidly, these systems are capable of identifying conditions at stages much earlier than traditional methods. The implications are profound, not just in terms of patient outcomes but also for healthcare cost management. The success here owes much to the startup's ability to collaborate closely with medical professionals and continually fine-tune their algorithms based on real-world data.

For those aspiring entrepreneurs and professionals considering similar applications of AI, these cases offer invaluable lessons. They each underscore the importance of robust partnerships and an agile approach to technology adoption. There's also an unmistakable element of customer-centric innovation. Businesses aren't just adopting AI; they're reconfiguring their entire customer interaction frameworks around AI capabilities.

What's particularly inspiring is that these success narratives are not confined to large corporations with vast resources. Even small businesses, equipped with the right strategy and technological tools, can and have achieved remarkable feats. A coffee chain that started as a local store is now setting industry standards by using AI to integrate its supply chain, manage inventory efficiently, and offer customers a personalized experience through a mobile app. The innovation lies not in having more, but in optimizing what's available.

These stories bring to light the critical role that agility and adaptability play in AI-driven business transformations. Entrepreneurs who succeed are those who are willing to pivot their strategies based on insights derived from AI analytics. There's a symbiotic relationship between technology and tactical business strategy, and it's this interplay that sets successful enterprises apart. Importantly, success doesn't merely happen; it is engineered through meticulous planning, iterative learning, and occasionally, calculated risk-taking.

In this digital age, it's inevitable that industries continuously evolve under the influence of AI technologies. Observing the transformative journeys of businesses already flourishing due to AI, we learn the substantial benefits of early adoption and innovation. A common denominator in these success stories is the relentless pursuit of knowledge — always staying a step ahead with the latest AI trends and tools.

Throughout these case studies, one can't dismiss the impact of leadership that's willing to embrace change and encourage a culture of innovation. Leaders who create an organizational environment that fosters creativity and technological adoption invariably find themselves at the forefront of industry evolution. This transformational culture often serves as the backbone for successful AI integration.

Finally, an essential aspect modern-day entrepreneurs can learn from these success stories is the importance of ethical AI practices. It's crucial to bridge the gap between technological advancement and moral responsibility, ensuring that AI deployments are transparent, fair, and non-discriminatory. Building trust through ethical use of AI strengthens brand reputation and promotes long-term success.

In conclusion, examining these success stories offers more than just admiration for what others have done. It provides a real, tangible roadmap for aspiring entrepreneurs looking to harness the power of AI. The paths may be unique, but the underlying principles remain the same: the thoughtful application of AI, a relentless commitment to innovation, and the courage to redefine traditional business paradigms. Real-life AI success stories are, without a doubt, the beacon that can guide future entrepreneurs toward their own financial growth and marketplace distinction.

Chapter 7:
Navigating AI Challenges and Risks

As you venture into the AI realm, navigating its challenges and risks becomes essential for leveraging its full potential for financial growth. Each step forward involves balancing innovation with caution, particularly when addressing ethical concerns and managing risks inherent in AI projects. Entrepreneurs, freelancers, and professionals must remain vigilant about AI's capabilities and limitations, ensuring transparency and adherence to ethical standards. Despite the complexities, engaging with AI responsibly can unlock significant opportunities. Developing robust risk management strategies not only protects your ventures but also builds trust with stakeholders and clients. By staying informed and proactive about the evolving AI landscape, you position yourself to harness its power responsibly and sustainably, ultimately leading to successful integration and financial achievements in your professional endeavors.

Addressing Ethical Concerns in AI

As we embrace the myriad possibilities AI offers, addressing ethical concerns becomes a pivotal aspect of integrating this technology into entrepreneurial ventures. AI must be developed and implemented with a steadfast commitment to fairness, transparency, and accountability. Entrepreneurs need to be acutely aware of issues like data privacy, algorithmic bias, and the societal impact of automation. By embedding ethical considerations into every stage of AI development, businesses can not only mitigate risks but also build trust with customers and stakeholders. This trust becomes a crucial factor in the sustainable growth of any AI-driven enterprise. Remember, responsible AI isn't just about compliance; it's about creating solutions that benefit both society and the bottom line.

Risk Management in AI Projects involves balancing innovation with responsibility. As entrepreneurs and professionals integrate AI into their operations, ethical considerations gain urgency. Balancing these ethical dimensions while managing risk can make or break an AI initiative.

The first step in risk management is understanding the inherent risks associated with AI. Ethical concerns often top this list. AI systems can inadvertently exhibit bias or lead to unintended discrimination. For instance, an AI hiring tool might favor certain demographics based on biased training data. If unchecked, such biases can lead to not only ethical dilemmas but also legal liabilities.

Addressing these concerns requires a proactive approach. Implementing a thorough risk assessment process is crucial. Entrepreneurs need to identify where biases might arise throughout an AI system's lifecycle—from data collection to algorithm deployment. Employing diverse teams to review and test AI systems can be an effective strategy to catch biases early.

Being aware of potential regulation changes is another essential element of risk management in AI. Various governments are starting to regulate AI more strictly, aiming to curb unethical uses. Keeping an eye on evolving laws ensures that AI projects remain compliant, avoiding costly penalties and preserving brand integrity.

Moreover, transparent communication is key. Clearly documenting how AI systems make decisions can alleviate stakeholder concerns. It's about building trust not only with customers but also with shareholders and regulators. Transparent systems foster trust and can be more easily integrated into enterprises, ensuring smooth implementation without reputational risks.

Risk management doesn't end with the initial implementation; it's an ongoing process. Regular audits and updates to the AI systems are necessary to mitigate risks associated with outdated protocols or emerging threats. The landscape of technology evolves, and AI systems must adapt to new developments and insights.

Considering cybersecurity risks is also essential. As AI systems become more embedded in operations, they can become targets for attacks. Securing AI systems against breaches protects not just sensitive data but also the company's reputation and bottom line. Incorporating strong encryption and regular security audits should be non-negotiable steps in risk management.

An effective way to manage AI risks is through scenario planning and stress testing. By simulating potential challenges AI systems might face, entrepreneurs can devise mitigation strategies. Exploring "what if" scenarios prepares the business for disruptions, minimizing impact and ensuring continuity.

Training and development shouldn't be overlooked. Ensuring that teams handling AI are well-versed in ethical implications and risk management is fundamental. Providing ongoing education programs about AI ethics and risk assessments empowers them to handle potential pitfalls dually with capability and confidence.

Involving all relevant stakeholders in the risk management process enriches the effort. Engaging legal, technical, and operational teams fosters a holistic understanding of an AI project's impact across different dimensions of the business.

Financial risk is another consideration. Investing in AI technology can entail significant expenses. Cost overruns, especially when adjusting systems post-implementation to address unforeseen ethical concerns, can strain resources. Proper budgeting and allocating funds for unforeseen issues preserve financial health.

Entrepreneurs should also consider partnerships with AI ethics experts or organizations specializing in ethical AI. These partnerships can provide insights and frameworks that help shape responsible AI use and outline paths for ethical processes that align with both organizational goals and societal expectations.

The multifaceted nature of AI risk management requires clarity of purpose and vision. Entrepreneurs must define what success looks like, not just in terms of performance metrics but also in ethical execution. By maintaining a commitment to ethical AI practices, they lay the foundations for sustainable, scalable projects that not only comply with current standards but also anticipate future demands.

Finally, sharing risk management experiences, both successes, and failures, within the AI community encourages collective learning and improvement. It's an ecosystem approach where shared knowledge fosters safer and more ethical AI evolution.

In conclusion, integrating AI successfully requires more than technological advancement; it's about evolving with a sense of responsibility. Risk management ensures that AI projects not only reach their potential for financial gain but do so in a way that respects and enhances the society they serve. As the landscape of AI continues to transform, effective risk management becomes a cornerstone of innovation with integrity.

Chapter 8:
AI Tools and Resources

In this chapter, we're delving into the diverse tools and resources that can accelerate your journey towards financial success with AI. Aspiring entrepreneurs and professionals will find insights on selecting cost-effective AI solutions that don't compromise on quality, helping you to work smarter, not harder. We highlight the value of open-source AI platforms, which offer accessible alternatives for those eager to innovate without the hefty price tag. These tools empower you to experiment and deploy AI solutions tailored to your unique needs and opportunities. By understanding and leveraging these resources, you'll be equipped to integrate AI seamlessly into your workflows, creating a robust foundation for financial growth. Ready to unlock the full potential of AI in your ventures? Let's get started with some game-changing tools and resources.

Cost-Effective AI Solutions

The landscape of AI presents an extraordinary opportunity to integrate impactful technologies without breaking the bank, especially for aspiring entrepreneurs and professionals keen on leveraging AI for financial growth. There are numerous cost-effective AI solutions available today, ranging from open source platforms to low-cost subscription services, enabling individuals and small businesses to access powerful tools once available only to larger players. By tapping into these resources, one can experiment, iterate, and innovate at a fraction of the traditional cost. It's essential to identify the right mix of tools that align with your specific goals and operational needs, which can unlock AI's potential to streamline operations, enhance productivity, and ultimately drive greater returns. Embracing these affordable solutions not only democratizes access to AI but also empowers users to harness the transformative effects of AI for competitive advantages in their respective fields.

Open Source AI Platforms are transforming how aspiring entrepreneurs, freelancers, and professionals can affordably harness the power of artificial intelligence. Open source AI tools offer a cost-effective solution to some of the barriers traditionally associated with implementing AI technology. You don't need a massive budget to explore AI's potential when a wide array of tools and resources are available right at your fingertips...

Open source AI platforms present a practical avenue for those who might otherwise be deterred by the high costs of proprietary software. These platforms often come with comprehensive documentation and an engaged community, offering support and encouragement to those willing to dive in. This collaborative environment not only reduces financial burden but also fosters the democratization of AI technologies, expanding accessibility beyond large corporations to individual innovators and small businesses.

Among the most well-known open-source AI platforms is TensorFlow, developed by Google Brain. This platform provides flexible tools for developing machine learning models. It's widely used by both beginners and experts, providing resources such as pre-configured models and extensive tutorials. TensorFlow's popularity is partly due to its vibrant community, which continuously contributes to improving both the platform itself and its ease of use.

Moreover, platforms like PyTorch, backed by Facebook's AI Research lab, offer another powerful tool for both academic research and developing commercial AI solutions. PyTorch is celebrated for its intuitive interface and dynamic computational graph, which allows for more flexible model building. PyTorch's framework supports GPU acceleration, making it suitable for demanding computational tasks while remaining accessible to those with fewer resources.

In addition to TensorFlow and PyTorch, other platforms like OpenAI GPT and Hugging Face have emerged as influential players in the open-source domain. These platforms focus on natural language processing, providing powerful pre-trained models that entrepreneurs and developers can adapt for various applications. For those looking to integrate AI-driven chatbots or language translators into their businesses, such tools offer a clear path with reduced overheads.

The open-source nature of these platforms implies ongoing updates and enhancements from a global community of users and developers. This collaborative innovation leads to rapid advancements and implementations across various industries—allowing even small-scale entrepreneurs to deploy sophisticated AI strategies that rivals might only dream of without hefty investments.

Many of these platforms also offer vast libraries of pre-existing models and datasets, which can greatly accelerate development times. For budding entrepreneurs and freelancers, saving time often translates directly into saving money, and the ability to quickly prototype and refine AI-driven solutions can offer a competitive edge. These aspects make them highly appealing for projects where time-to-market could determine the difference between success and failure.

An often overlooked aspect of utilizing open-source platforms is the educational value they bring. Aspiring professionals integrate these tools into their work, gaining hands-on experience which translates into valuable skills in the broader job market. This learning component is invaluable, as it empowers users not just to use AI but to truly understand and create with it, ultimately opening doors to new opportunities and financial growth.

Nevertheless, integrating open-source AI isn't without its challenges. Users should be aware of the technical expertise required to effectively leverage these tools. It may take some time to grasp their full potential, but the investment in learning pays dividends. Resources like online forums, user groups, and open-source community events provide invaluable support and knowledge-sharing opportunities.

When considering the implementation of open-source AI tools, it's crucial to factor in the licensing agreements associated with these platforms. While these tools are generally free, understanding the legal aspects of their use ensures compliance and helps mitigate any potential risks in commercial deployments.

The potential open-source AI holds is only limited by imagination and willingness to explore. The collaborative spirit inherent in open-source communities continues to fuel innovation and accessibility, enabling a wider range of people to partake in AI's transformative capabilities. By leveraging these platforms, entrepreneurs and freelancers can explore, iterate, and implement solutions that are both revolutionary and financially viable.

For those about to embark on the journey of integrating open-source AI platforms into their work, remember, it's not just about saving costs. It's about seizing the opportunity to engage with a community, often resulting in innovations that exceed their own expectations. Through tenacity and collaboration, the door to AI-fueled growth and success swings wide open.

Chapter 9:
Building AI-Enabled Teams

Transitioning to an AI-enabled team requires more than just hiring the right talent—it's about fostering a culture that embraces innovation and continuously adapts to new technologies. Begin by identifying roles where AI can optimize processes or unlock new potential, then seek individuals who not only possess technical skills but also demonstrate a keen ability to collaborate and problem-solve creatively. Emphasize the importance of cross-functional understanding; team members need to communicate effectively across disciplines to integrate AI solutions seamlessly. Encourage ongoing learning and development to stay ahead of AI advancements, ensuring your team doesn't just use AI but builds upon it to drive growth and innovation. Remember, the goal is to weave AI into the fabric of your team's daily operations, transforming challenges into opportunities and technology into tangible results.

Recruiting AI Talent

When you're on a quest to build a powerhouse AI-enabled team, bringing in the right talent is absolutely crucial to setting a strong foundation. It's not just about assembling a group with impressive resumes; it's about identifying individuals whose skills and mindsets align seamlessly with your team's goals. You need people who are not only proficient in AI technologies but are also adaptable, eager to learn, and can contribute to a culture of innovation. Emphasize recruiting diverse expertise, blending roles such as data scientists, machine learning engineers, and business strategists, ensuring they complement each other and drive your AI initiatives forward. Look for candidates who are not only technically adept but can also communicate complex AI concepts in simple terms, thus bridging the gap between tech and non-tech team members. In this way, you're setting your business up to navigate the ever-evolving AI landscape with agility and foresight.

Preparing Teams for AI Integration As we delve deeper into the process of building AI-enabled teams, preparing your existing team for AI integration becomes an indispensable step. The era of AI isn't a distant future; it's unfolding as we speak. And preparing your team effectively can spell the difference between seamlessly integrating AI and facing significant resistance or obstacles. Let's explore concrete steps to equip your teams for AI's promising yet complex landscape.

Start with communication. Clear and open dialogue about why AI integration is being pursued can dissolve any misconceptions and fears of displacement. Explain the vision behind AI adoption and how it aligns with your overall organizational goals. This transparency can foster an environment of trust and excitement rather than apprehension. Remember, it's not just about selling the benefits but also addressing concerns candidly.

Another key step is to create a culture of learning. Encourage curiosity and continuous education about AI. Some team members might be tech-savvy, others not so much. Offering training sessions, workshops, and even digital courses can level the playing field and empower everyone to engage with AI technology confidently. This investment in knowledge will serve your team in the long run, making them adaptable and innovative in their roles.

Reframing roles is another aspect of preparation. AI can handle routine tasks efficiently, freeing up human talent for more strategic, creative, and decision-oriented duties. Work with your team to realign roles and responsibilities, emphasizing how AI tools can enhance, not replace, their contributions. This collaborative approach can invigorate team spirit, as employees see themselves growing alongside technology rather than being overshadowed by it.

Encouraging collaboration between AI specialists and existing team members is equally vital. Often, AI adoption is perceived as a division between 'us' and 'them'—the tech experts versus everyone else. Breaking down these silos can be achieved by fostering collaborative projects and informal networking opportunities where knowledge exchange flows naturally. Such interactions can demystify AI, fostering a hybrid team capable of leveraging diverse skills.

Feedback loops are essential. Create mechanisms for regular feedback on the AI integration process. These can be informal meetings, suggestion boxes, or anonymous surveys. Listening to your team's feedback allows you to course-correct and make necessary adjustments. It also acknowledges the human element in AI integration, ensuring that technology serves people, not the other way around.

It's also important to set reasonable expectations. AI transformation doesn't occur overnight. Conveying achievable milestones can celebrate progress without setting unreasonable targets. This gradual approach can keep morale high and maintain momentum throughout the transition.

Investing in tools and infrastructure is non-negotiable. AI integration may require enhancements in your tech ecosystem to manage new processes efficiently. Ensure your organization is well-equipped with the necessary hardware and software. This investment underscores your commitment to optimizing AI usage, laying a strong foundation for future innovation.

Don't neglect the importance of ethical training. The development and deployment of AI come with ethical considerations. Training your team to recognize and handle ethical dilemmas fosters responsible AI use and positions your organization as a leader in ethical AI practices. This prepares your team to navigate the nuanced AI landscape effectively and responsibly.

Your aim should be to cultivate an environment where change is seen as an opportunity rather than a threat. The dynamic nature of AI requires agility, resilience, and a willingness to embrace new paradigms. By equipping your team with the right tools, mindset, and support, you'll position them to thrive amid AI advancements. Through effective preparation, you'll foster a team that's not just ready for AI integration but one that's excited to be part of AI-driven innovation.

Chapter 10:
Marketing and Selling AI Solutions

In the world of AI, having an innovative product is only half the battle; the real challenge lies in effectively marketing and selling these solutions to a discerning audience. To stand out in a competitive landscape, aspiring entrepreneurs and professionals must tailor their marketing strategies to highlight the unique benefits and real-world applications of their AI offerings. It's essential to craft compelling narratives that resonate with potential customers, emphasizing the value propositions that AI brings to their everyday challenges. Building trust is crucial; transparency about how AI models work, addressing data privacy concerns, and showcasing successful case studies can reassure skeptical clients. Moreover, leveraging multiple channels for product promotion—be it digital campaigns, webinars, or industry conferences—can maximize outreach. By focusing on clear communication, ethical practices, and customer-centric solutions, you can transform AI innovations into profitable ventures.

Effective AI Product Launch Strategies

Launching an AI product requires a blend of strategic thinking, market understanding, and customer engagement. First, it's crucial to have a deep insight into your target audience and the unique value your product brings to them. Conduct thorough market research to position your AI solution effectively, highlighting how it solves customer pain points better than existing alternatives. Building a robust pre-launch strategy that involves buzz generation, such as teaser campaigns and influencer collaborations, can create anticipation and excitement. Next, ensure that your launch is an event, both virtual and in-person, that showcases the product's capabilities through live demonstrations and customer testimonials. Engage with your audience through interactive sessions to address questions and gather feedback, fostering a community around your product. Finally, leveraging data analytics is vital to refine your post-launch strategies, allowing for agile adjustments to marketing tactics based on user behavior and feedback, ensuring your AI product not only meets expectations but exceeds them.

Building Customer Trust in AI One of the most crucial elements of launching an AI product successfully is ensuring that customers trust what you're selling. Trust is not a one-time deal—it's something that's built over time through transparency, reliability, and empathy. This is particularly important in the realm of AI, where apprehensions about data security, ethical concerns, and the fear of the unknown can make potential customers hesitant. Effective communication and presentation can alleviate these concerns and cement trust during an AI product launch.

Start by being transparent about how your AI product works. Consumers are becoming increasingly savvy and want to know what's happening behind the scenes. Provide clear information on data usage, how algorithms function, and what security measures are in place to protect user data. This isn't just about listing features; it's about educating your audience in a way that empowers them to feel comfortable using your product. The more informed they are, the more likely they are to trust your innovation.

An essential part of building trust revolves around demonstrating the value your AI solution offers. Clearly articulate the problems it solves and the tangible benefits it provides. Case studies or white papers that show the AI in action can serve as powerful tools. Real-world examples highlight your product's efficacy and give potential customers the assurance they need that what you're offering is both legitimate and beneficial.

User testimonials are another key element in establishing trust. Encourage satisfied customers to share their experiences. Honest reviews can be far more effective than even the most polished marketing campaign. When people see that others have found value in your product, it creates a sense of community and reliability. Word-of-mouth remains an incredibly powerful form of marketing, particularly in disruptive fields like AI.

Maintaining open channels of communication is also vital. Prioritize customer service and be accessible to address queries, concerns, or feedback promptly. This interaction can humanize your AI product, creating a rapport with your audience. Listening to customer feedback also offers valuable insights into how your product is being received and could highlight areas for improvement.

Security concerns commonly arise when discussing AI. Proactively addressing these issues can set your product apart. Highlight the security protocols in place and provide regular updates on how the company is advancing them. Data protection is an ongoing process, and letting your customers know you value their privacy can significantly enhance their trust in your product.

Another aspect of building trust involves humanizing your brand. People are more likely to trust a company that shows there are real, empathetic humans behind the technology. Share stories about your team, your company's mission, and the values that drive your product development. This transparency not only builds trust but can also foster customer loyalty.

Finally, be genuine about limitations. No AI solution is perfect, and being upfront about your product's challenges shows integrity. By acknowledging areas where improvement is needed, you can preemptively address potential customer frustrations and demonstrate a commitment to ongoing development. This honesty doesn't weaken your brand; on the contrary, it elevates it.

As you prepare to launch your AI product, remember that trust isn't just a checkbox on a to-do list—it's an ongoing journey. With careful, thoughtful strategies for communication, transparency, and relationship-building, you can establish a customer base that not only trusts your product but also becomes loyal advocates for your brand.

Chapter 11:
Future Trends in AI

As we turn our focus to the future, the landscape of AI is set to evolve with unprecedented innovations that promise to redefine industries and workplace dynamics. From the adoption of AI-enhanced personalization to the expansion of autonomous systems, businesses and professionals must keep a keen eye on these developments. Embracing the shift towards explainable AI and ethical considerations will not only foster trust but also spur creative solutions tailored to user needs. The challenge and opportunity lie in understanding these emerging trends to adapt quickly, ensuring that you position yourself strategically for the forthcoming wave of AI revolutions. The clarity, agility, and foresight you cultivate now will form the foundation for seizing the financial benefits AI's future holds.

Predicting the Next Wave of AI Innovations

The future of AI holds boundless opportunities, and being able to predict the next wave of innovations could be the key to staying ahead in a rapidly evolving market. Aspiring entrepreneurs and professionals should look at AI technologies like machine learning, natural language processing, and robotics as the building blocks for groundbreaking solutions that will disrupt industries. But it doesn't stop at just understanding the technology; it's about envisioning creative applications that solve real-world problems and anticipating changes in customer needs and market dynamics. In doing so, you'll not only position yourself at the forefront of innovation but also empower your business to leverage AI for unprecedented financial growth. Now's the time to embrace a forward-thinking mindset, eager to seize new opportunities that are on the horizon.

Positioning for Future Success requires foresight, adaptability, and a strategic mindset. As we look to the future of AI, it's clear that the landscape will continue to evolve rapidly. Entrepreneurs, freelancers, and professionals eager to integrate AI into their work for financial growth must anticipate the next wave of innovations while preparing to seize the opportunities these changes will bring. This doesn't mean just keeping up; it means staying ahead.

First, envision future AI innovations through the lens of emerging technologies. As AI technology matures, it will undoubtedly intersect with other cutting-edge fields like quantum computing, biotechnology, and augmented reality. By identifying intersections and understanding how AI can enhance these technologies, you can position yourself as a thought leader in your industry. This requires not only technical knowledge but also the ability to foresee market demands and societal trends that might influence the adoption of such innovations.

Moreover, fostering a culture of continuous learning and adaptability is crucial. The AI landscape is highly dynamic, with new tools, frameworks, and methodologies emerging at a breakneck pace. Entrepreneurs and professionals who prioritize learning and adaptability will find themselves better positioned to identify and harness these new tools. Engage with online AI courses, workshops, and hackathons to stay updated. Networking with other AI professionals and thought leaders can provide invaluable insights into new trends and potential applications.

In a world where AI is ubiquitous, differentiation becomes key. To stand out in a crowded market, focus on developing niche applications of AI tailored to specific industries or consumer needs. Whether it's an AI-driven solution for healthcare diagnostics or a personalized AI marketing tool, niche applications can provide a competitive edge. This specificity not only adds value but also addresses particular pain points, making your AI solution indispensable to your target audience.

Investing strategically in AI research and development can't be overstated. Allocate resources to explore new AI models and algorithms that promise efficiency and novel applications. An emphasis on R&D will ensure that you are always contributing to cutting-edge solutions and staying relevant as the technology landscape shifts. Innovation is at its peak when there's a support system encouraging exploration and experimentation without the fear of failure.

Collaboration will be a cornerstone of positioning for future success as well. The complexity and scale of AI projects often require multidisciplinary expertise. Partnering with domain experts can enrich your AI solutions with specialized knowledge, facilitating more informed and effective applications. Collaborations with academia, startups, and tech giants can also offer access to resources and tools that might otherwise be out of reach, accelerating your path to innovation.

Don't underestimate the power of ethical considerations in positioning for future success. As AI becomes more ingrained in society, ethical concerns will loom large. Technologies that responsibly and transparently address issues such as data privacy, bias, and AI decision-making processes will gain consumer trust and loyalty more easily. Embedding ethical principles into your AI projects will differentiate your solutions and align them with societal values, crucial for long-term acceptance and success.

Furthermore, public perception and regulatory landscapes will shape the future of AI. Stay informed about regulatory changes and anticipate how these may affect the deployment of AI technologies. Legal considerations will increasingly influence project feasibility, particularly with regard to data handling and algorithmic transparency. By aligning your strategies with existing and upcoming regulations, you'll minimize risks and build trust with clients and stakeholders.

Fostering an environment of innovation involves not just technological advancements but also effective leadership and vision. Leaders who embrace a forward-thinking approach and encourage their teams to push the boundaries of what's possible will be at the forefront of AI advancement. By nurturing a team culture that supports creative thinking and rewards innovative ideas, businesses can successfully navigate the challenges of the future AI landscape.

Equally important is the ability to scale effectively. As AI technologies advance, having the infrastructure to scale solutions rapidly will be paramount. Building scalable systems from the outset ensures that as demand grows, your solutions can adapt without sacrificing performance or user satisfaction. Cloud computing, for example, provides scalable resources to accommodate ever-changing demands, offering a flexible solution for growing and maintaining complex AI applications.

Ultimately, positioning for future success within the AI realm encompasses a holistic approach. From continuous learning and strategic investment to ethical considerations and effective scaling, each element plays a crucial role in navigating the next wave of AI innovations. By embracing these strategies, aspiring entrepreneurs, freelancers, and professionals are better prepared to leverage AI not just for financial gain but for creating profound and lasting impacts across industries.

Chapter 12:
AI for Financial Growth

In the dynamic world of AI, seizing financial opportunities involves a blend of smart strategies and relentless innovation. For entrepreneurs, freelancers, and professionals eager to harness AI for financial gain, understanding the evolving landscape is crucial. AI is reshaping financial services by optimizing investment portfolios, automating routine tasks, and offering predictive analytics that can drive informed decision-making. This horizon presents diverse investment opportunities—from backing AI-focused startups to integrating AI solutions into existing business models. Unlocking these potentials requires not just adopting AI tools but strategically aligning them with clear financial goals. As AI technologies advance, the potential for maximizing returns grows exponentially, offering a fertile ground for those who adapt swiftly and innovate continuously. Embracing AI for financial growth isn't a mere option anymore; it's a pathway to staying competitive and thriving in the modern economy.

Strategies for Maximizing Returns

To effectively maximize returns when integrating AI into your work, it's crucial to develop a keen understanding of both market demands and technological capabilities. Start by identifying areas where AI can provide the most value, such as automating mundane tasks, enhancing decision-making processes, or personalizing customer experiences. Evaluate the potential return on investment (ROI) by analyzing various AI-driven solutions and their long-term benefits. It's important to remain agile, embracing new advancements and refining your approach as technology evolves. Moreover, diversifying AI applications across multiple facets of your business can mitigate risks and capitalize on different revenue streams. Finally, surrounding yourself with a team that shares your vision and is proficient in AI will further ensure that your AI strategy is robust and scalable. With the right approach, AI has the potential to transform financial growth from just an aspiration into a sustainable reality.

Investment Opportunities in AI are vast and varied, providing a fertile ground for those looking to maximize returns in a rapidly advancing technological landscape. As we dive deeper into the realm of AI for financial growth, it's crucial to identify and understand these opportunities that hold immense potential for savvy investors and entrepreneurs alike.

In the last decade, AI has transitioned from a futuristic concept to a pivotal component in various industries. This shift has ignited a flood of investment opportunities, driving the creation of AI-focused startups, innovative products, and cutting-edge services. Understanding where to place your investments efficiently can lead to significant financial returns, especially for those aiming to stay ahead of the curve. The key lies in recognizing the sectors where AI is not just useful, but transformative.

One of the most promising areas for investment is AI-driven automation. Automation using AI technology has revolutionized industries such as manufacturing, finance, and healthcare by streamlining processes and minimizing errors. Investors can look at businesses that offer AI-based automation solutions as there is a growing demand for systems that can reduce operational costs and improve efficiency. Companies that are developing machine learning algorithms to enhance automation capabilities continue to attract significant interest from venture capitalists and other investors.

Financial technology, or FinTech, represents another lucrative investment avenue. AI enhances capabilities in risk assessment, fraud detection, and personalized financial advice. By enhancing these essential services, AI has created numerous opportunities for investors to back startups and established companies that incorporate such technologies. FinTech firms that leverage AI for predictive analytics and improve customer service platforms often stand out as high-potential investments.

Moreover, the healthcare sector is ripe with opportunities, particularly in areas like medical imaging and personalized medicine. AI algorithms can analyze vast amounts of data to assist in early diagnosis, patient management, and treatment planning. By investing in AI healthcare startups or established companies innovating in this space, investors can contribute to and benefit from advancements that promise to revolutionize patient care while generating significant returns.

AI's presence in the consumer sector cannot be overlooked. From AI-powered voice assistants to smart home devices, the consumer market is rapidly growing. Companies that design and implement AI for everyday convenience, personalization, and security present ample opportunities for investment. These products are not only enhancing user experience but are also setting new standards in the tech industry, making them attractive targets for investors looking for long-term growth.

Education technology, or EdTech, is another burgeoning sector where AI's potential is being harnessed. From adaptive learning platforms that tailor educational content to individual learners to AI-driven administrative tools that streamline school operations, there are numerous opportunities to support startups focused on reshaping the education landscape. This is particularly vital as traditional educational models are being challenged by the need for more personalized and flexible learning experiences.

Understanding and navigating the legal and ethical implications of AI is crucial when considering investments. As AI technologies continue to evolve, they're increasingly scrutinized for potential biases and ethical concerns. Investments in companies that prioritize ethical AI development and include explainability features in their solutions are not only more sustainable but also appealing to stakeholders mindful of regulatory and social issues.

A strategic approach to identifying investment opportunities involves conducting thorough market research to understand current trends, potential disruptions, and emerging technologies. Engaging with professionals and leveraging networks within the AI field can offer valuable insights and guidance. Attending tech conferences, participating in startup incubators, and subscribing to specialized AI publications can also be instrumental in staying informed and making educated investment decisions.

Diversification remains a fundamental principle for any investment strategy. Within the AI space, spreading investments across different sectors and stages—whether they're nascent startups or established companies—can mitigate risk and maximize potential returns. While early-stage startups might offer high-reward possibilities, they also come with higher risks. In contrast, investing in a well-established AI company might yield more modest yet steadier returns.

Finally, partnerships and collaborations can be a powerful means to tap into AI investment opportunities. Collaborating with tech companies, research institutions, and even governments can open doors to exclusive projects and initiatives. Such collaborations not only broaden an investor's scope but also provide a deeper understanding of the industry's direction and challenges.

As you consider venturing into AI investments, remember that the true value lies not just in the present technology but in its potential to reshape industries and create new markets. The leaders of tomorrow in AI investment will be those who understand its transformative capabilities and invest strategically, balancing innovation with practicality, and opportunity with risk. By embracing a vision that looks beyond immediate gains, you set the stage for long-term, sustainable financial success.

Conclusion

As we've journeyed through the dynamic landscape of artificial intelligence, it's evident that AI holds unprecedented potential for driving financial success across various fields. Aspiring entrepreneurs, freelancers, and professionals now find themselves at the cusp of a technological revolution that possesses the power to transform how they work, innovate, and create value. The insights drawn from the preceding chapters highlight the myriad of opportunities that AI presents, alongside the challenges that must be navigated with care and foresight.

AI's capacity to automate repetitive tasks and enable data-driven decision-making is only just the beginning. With a profound understanding of key AI components, professionals can harness algorithms' transformative capabilities and apply them to real-world problems. The distinction between machine learning and deep learning further emphasizes the versatility of AI technologies, catering to specific needs and enhancing various business processes. This knowledge sets the foundation for more informed strategic decisions and opens avenues for profitable ventures.

For entrepreneurs, the AI startup environment is vibrant and filled with promise. By analyzing case studies of successful AI startups, it's clear that agility, innovation, and a customer-centric approach are critical in crafting solutions that stand out. Lessons learned from these pioneers offer a roadmap for emerging businesses aiming to carve their niches in the competitive AI sector. The continuous evolution of products and services, bolstered by smart monetization strategies, solidifies the role of AI in shaping tomorrow's enterprises.

Freelancers, now more than ever, have the tools to redefine their careers through AI-enhanced methodologies. Integrating AI tools not only maximizes productivity but also redefines how freelancers approach their work, saving time and allowing focus on more strategic endeavors. This paradigm shift in freelancing brings about greater freedom and flexibility while ensuring a competitive edge in the marketplace.

Professional development is significantly augmented by AI, as individuals not only gain access to cutting-edge online AI courses but also enhance their skill sets in ways that would have been unimaginable just a decade ago. Staying abreast of advancements in AI equips professionals with the tools they need to maintain relevance and thrive in an ever-evolving workforce.

Success stories from AI innovators illuminate the path forward, providing tangible examples of how AI has transformed businesses across sectors. These narratives do more than inspire; they serve as a blueprint for practical application, highlighting the importance of strategic thinking, adaptive learning, and resilience.

The challenges and risks associated with AI cannot be overlooked. Addressing ethical concerns and managing risk in AI projects are crucial for sustainable development. Entrepreneurs and professionals must cultivate a deep understanding of these elements to navigate the AI terrain responsibly, balancing innovation with integrity.

Access to cost-effective AI tools and open-source platforms democratizes AI, leveling the playing field for startups and established businesses alike. These resources empower individuals to experiment, iterate, and innovate without considerable financial constraints.

Building AI-enabled teams is more than just recruiting talent; it's about preparing teams for seamless AI integration. This involves fostering a culture of continuous learning and adaptability, ensuring that teams are equipped to meet the challenges and opportunities presented by AI head-on.

Marketing and selling AI solutions effectively require a deep understanding of consumer needs and the ability to build trust. By leveraging strategic launch techniques and robust customer relationship management, businesses can ensure their AI solutions resonate with target audiences.

Looking towards the future, AI's evolution is brimming with potential. By positioning themselves strategically, businesses and individuals can capitalize on emerging trends and innovations. This forward-thinking approach not only secures future success but also ensures continuous relevance in a rapidly changing landscape.

In conclusion, AI is not merely a tool—it's a catalyst for change and a beacon for financial growth in the modern era. While the journey is filled with complexities, the potential gains are immense for those willing to embrace AI's transformative power. As the future unfolds, the stories of success will belong to those who are visionary, informed, and unafraid to push the limits of what AI can achieve. With determination and the right strategies, financial growth through AI is not just a possibility; it's an inevitable reality for those who choose to embark on this journey.

Additional Resources and Glossary

In this section, we'll delve into some key terms and resources that will serve as valuable tools on your journey to integrating AI into your professional endeavors. Understanding these concepts is crucial to leveraging AI effectively and ethically.

Glossary Terms

Algorithm: A set of rules or steps used by computers to perform tasks. In AI, algorithms help machines learn from data and make decisions.

Automation: The technique of making processes operate automatically, often through AI, to increase efficiency and reduce the need for human intervention.

Deep Learning: A subset of machine learning that uses neural networks with many layers ("deep" layers) to analyze various factors of data.

Machine Learning: A type of AI that enables computers to learn from data and improve over time without being explicitly programmed.

Monetization Strategies: Techniques and business models used to generate revenue from AI-driven products and services.

Neural Networks: Computing systems inspired by the human brain's network of neurons, used in machine learning for pattern recognition.

Open Source: Software with source code that anyone can inspect, modify, and enhance. Open-source AI platforms are cost-effective tools for developing AI solutions.

Risk Management: The process of identifying, assessing, and controlling threats to an organization's capital and earnings, especially important in AI projects.

Additional Resources

Online AI Courses: Platforms like Coursera, edX, and Udacity offer comprehensive courses to help you elevate your AI skills from beginner to advanced levels.

AI Community Forums: Engaging in online communities such as Reddit's Machine Learning subreddit or AI-focused groups on LinkedIn can provide valuable insights and networking opportunities.

AI Research Papers: Websites like arXiv.org publish papers that can give you a deeper understanding of the latest in AI research and development.

AI Conferences: Attending events such as the AI Expo or the International Conference on Machine Learning offers exposure to cutting-edge technologies and industry networking.

By familiarizing yourself with these terms and utilizing the suggested resources, you'll be well-prepared to navigate the complex yet rewarding landscape of AI. Let this glossary be a springboard to further exploration and learning, empowering you to harness AI for financial success and innovation.